COMMUNICATION

Keith Wicks

Macdonald Educational

How to use this book

First, look at the contents page opposite. Read the chapter list to see if it includes the subject you want. The list tells you what each page is about. You can then find the page with the information you need.

If you want to know about one particular thing, look it up in the index on page 31. For example, if you want to know about writing, the index tells you that there is something about it on page 8. The index also lists the pictures in the book.

When you read this book, you will find some unusual words. The glossary on page 30 explains what they mean.

Series Editor
Margaret Conroy

Book Editor
Suzanne Greene

Factual adviser
John Stevenson

Reading consultant
Amy Gibbs
Inner London Education Authority
Centre for Language in Primary
Education

Series Design
Robert Mathias/Anne Isseyegh

Book Design
Anne Isseyegh/Jane Robison

Production
Susan Mead

Picture Research
Kathy Lockley

Teacher panel
Catherine Daniel, Lynn McCoombe,
Joanne Waterhouse

Illustrations
Dave Eaton Front cover
David Bryant/Joan Farmer Artists
Pages 16-17, 22-23, 24-25
Jeremy Gower/B.L. Kearley Ltd
Pages 12-13, 20-21
Gary Rees/Linda Rogers Associates
Pages 6-7, 8-9, 18-19, 28-29

Photographs
Aldus Archive/Fiona Pragoff: cover BR
Heather Angel/Biofotos: 10
BBC TV: 14
Sally & Richard Greenhill: 22
Robert Harding Picture Library: 11B
Imperial War Museum: 17
London Features International: 15
NASA: 26, 27
The Post Office: 25
ZEFA: cover L & TR, 9, 11T

CONTENTS

BASIC COMMUNICATION

Why we communicate

Communication means the sending of a message from one place to another. People communicate nearly all the time, for example we often want to tell each other when we are hungry, in pain, or need something.

Talking is an important way of communicating. We can communicate ideas and feelings in words as well as giving information. This usually makes life more interesting and enjoyable.

Even when people are not actually speaking, the way they look or behave can still tell us things about them. For example, a smile tells us that they are happy, and a frown tells us that they are worried or angry.

Homes are filled with many things that help us communicate. How many can you see in this picture?

6

There are many other ways of communicating. Clocks, pictures and many of the things we have around us have been made by people in order to tell us something. There are machines that can send messages to the other side of the world, or even out into Space.

How we communicate

You can easily give information to other people by talking to them. But you also use your body to communicate. For example, by shaking your head you are saying 'no', and by hunching up your shoulders and pressing your lips together you show that you are sulking.

Humans can give out information by what they wear. A uniform can tell us what job somebody does, and clothes can tell us what sort of country someone lives in. The way somebody dresses can give us an idea of what they are like. For example, their clothes may be neat and sensible, or very bright and striking. We may think that someone's personality is shown by the way they dress.

Writing things down is a good way of giving information because the message lasts for a long time. More people can read the information, especially if the message is put in a place where everyone can see it, or if there are lots of copies. You write things down at school to make a note of what you have heard, or to show the teacher what you have learned.

Signs give useful information, such as the names of streets, the kind of product a shop sells, or how far it is to another town. They are usually put where many people can see them.

Flags, symbols, and clothes give us information. What do the people's clothes tell you about them? Where are the telephones?

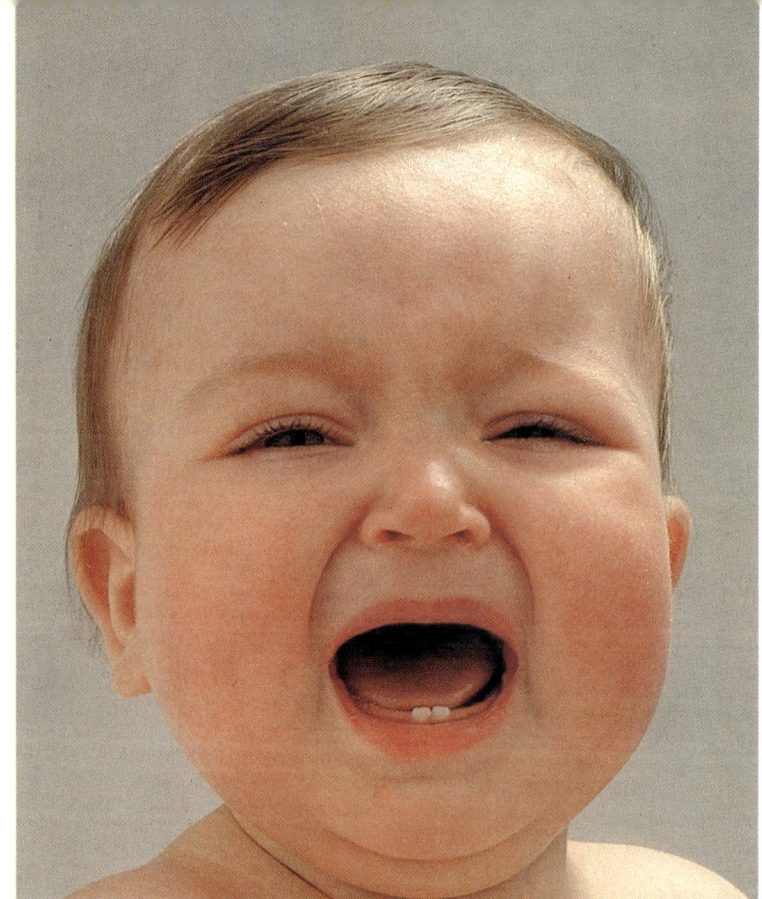

Before they can talk, babies use simple ways of telling us how they feel. How do you think this baby was feeling when the photograph was taken?

At an airport or a large station, simple symbols are used instead of words, so people from any country can understand what they mean. The next time you go to a station or airport, see how many signs you can spot. Are their meanings clear? If not, try to make up some better signs that everyone can understand. Then try them out on your friends and see if your signs give the right messages.

9

Animal communication

Like humans, animals need to communicate with one another. An animal will often make a sound to warn others of danger. For example, many birds make alarm calls when they are in danger. Animals also make sounds to tell others whether they are male or female, and so attract a partner.

Animals have other ways of communicating. A bee can tell members of its hive where it has found food by performing a dance. From the pattern of the dance and the way the bee wiggles, the others can tell the direction of the food and how far away it is.

This red frog from South America is poisonous. Animals that eat frogs soon learn that red frogs taste bad. So the colour communicates the warning 'bad to eat', and helps to protect the frog from its enemies.

Colour is important in animal communication. The brightly coloured feathers on some birds help them to attract a partner. But many insects have bright colours or strong patterns that stop other animals from trying to eat them. If one insect with a certain pattern has a bad taste, its enemies soon learn not to eat any more with the same pattern. Poisonous frogs and other animals that taste bad are often brightly coloured. This kind of protection is called warning coloration.

Animals can communicate with humans. We can teach animals to obey simple orders. And pets soon find ways of letting their owners know when they want food, or need to go outside.

An orang utan bares its teeth to show that it is angry and may bite.

A male frog fills his air sac so that he seems larger than he actually is. This helps him to frighten off enemies.

REACHING MANY

Printed words

Books, newspapers and magazines all use words and pictures to communicate. You can read the information that they give as slowly or as quickly as you like. If you forget something that you have read, you can look it up and read it again. Books are usually strongly made, so that people can keep them for a long time.

It may take an author many months to write a book. Then several more months pass before the book is printed and appears in the shops. This delay does not matter with story books or some information books. Other books, however, can soon become out-of-date. In science, for example, people are finding out important new things all the time. So you have to get the latest information from other sorts of communication, such as television and radio.

pasting down the proofs in position on the page

proofs

typing up the story

developing the photograph

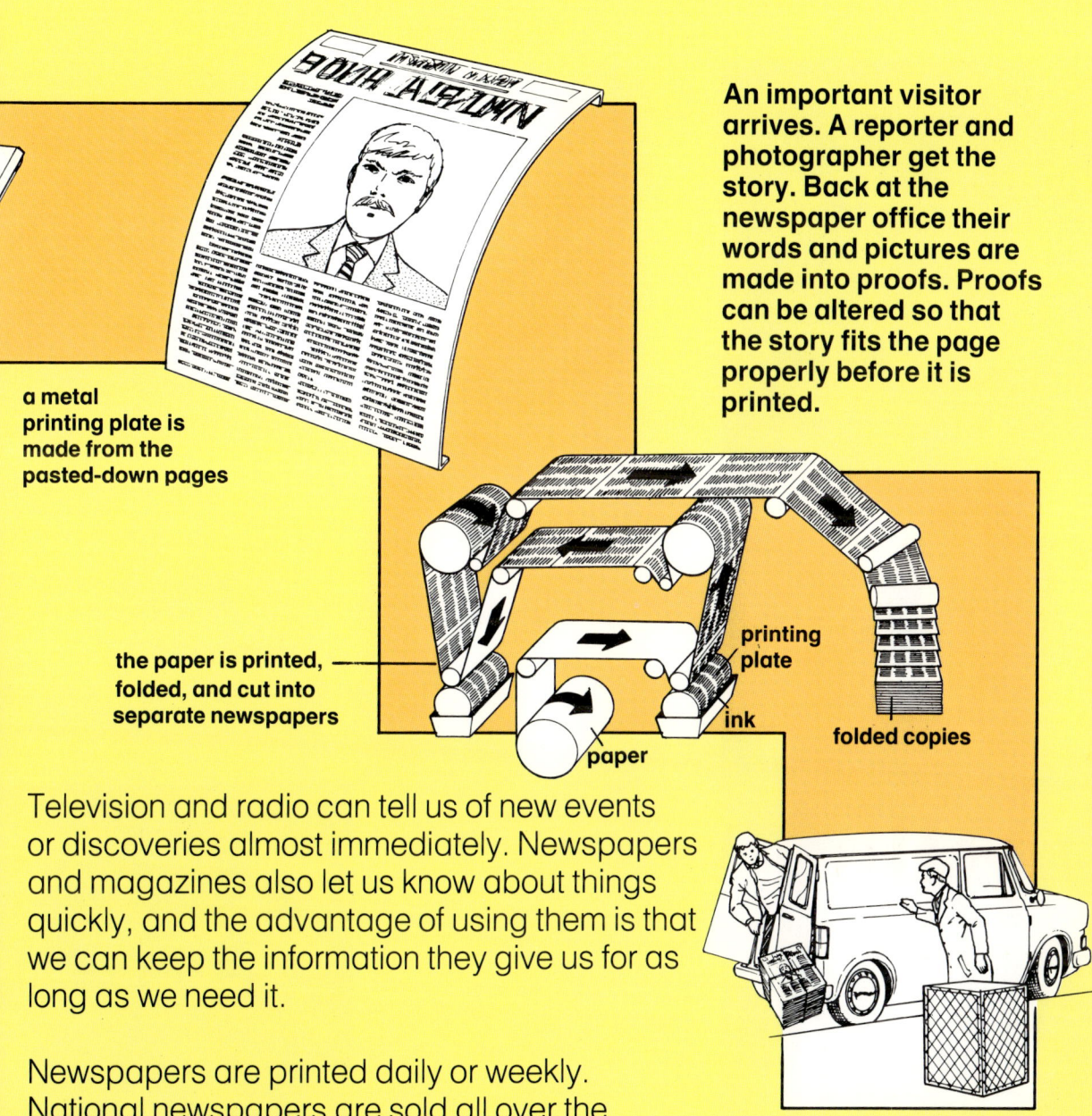

a metal printing plate is made from the pasted-down pages

An important visitor arrives. A reporter and photographer get the story. Back at the newspaper office their words and pictures are made into proofs. Proofs can be altered so that the story fits the page properly before it is printed.

the paper is printed, folded, and cut into separate newspapers

printing plate

ink

paper

folded copies

Television and radio can tell us of new events or discoveries almost immediately. Newspapers and magazines also let us know about things quickly, and the advantage of using them is that we can keep the information they give us for as long as we need it.

Newspapers are printed daily or weekly. National newspapers are sold all over the country, and tell us what has happened in our country and the world. Local newspapers tell us about events in the area that we live in. Magazines usually give information about one particular subject, such as gardening or sport. They are mostly printed weekly or monthly.

A van rushes the newspapers to the local shops and street sellers

13

Entertainment

Most forms of entertainment also communicate ideas to us. For example, the people who make television series about cowboys or detectives usually try to give the simple message that people who do wrong are punished in the end. So you can usually guess what will happen at the end of this kind of film.

This is a good message, but sometimes a bad message can be given out by accident. For example, people may get the idea from some films that it is all right to take violent revenge on those who have done wrong.

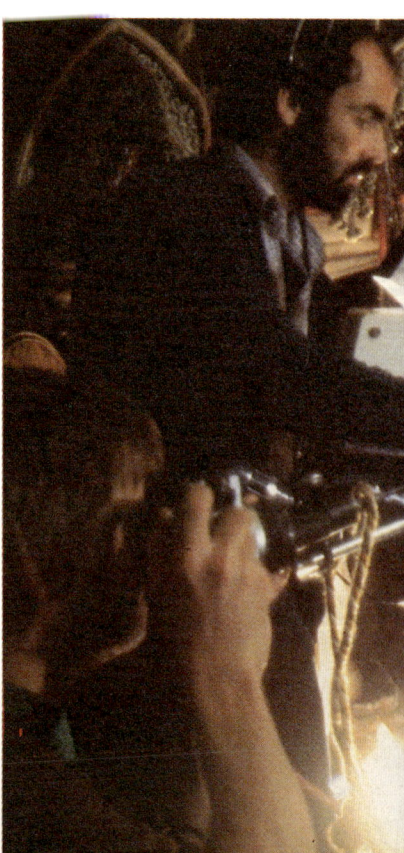

Michael Jackson is a singer and dancer who is very famous in the United States and much of Europe. Why do you think he is so popular?

The ideas communicated by films may be more powerful than you realise. After watching Superman, children have hurt themselves trying to copy their hero. So warnings are sometimes given to stop children from trying to fly!

To be successful on stage, a performer needs to communicate with the audience. Sometimes the songs may communicate strong feelings or ideas that the audience can easily understand.

Think of your favourite pop star. Just what is it that you like so much? It may be the sound, but often the performer communicates the sort of personality that the audience likes or admires. This is why some people try to behave or dress like their favourite star.

These people are recording a television programme based on a well-known English novel, 'The Mayor of Casterbridge'. The programme entertains us with its attractive costumes and scenery, while passing on to us the ideas of the author.

Power of persuasion

People are always trying to persuade us to do something. You probably have your own ways of trying to get people to do what you want! Companies that sell products, such as chocolate or cars, need to persuade people to buy them. One of the most powerful ways of doing this is by advertising. This can take many forms, such as printed words and pictures, or radio and television advertisements.

Television has persuaded this boy that he must have a certain toy. But can he persuade his father to buy it?

Some advertisements give us a clear message that a certain product is the best. Others try to show that people who look happy and successful use a certain product. If we believe this, we may think that if we use the same product, we will also become happy and successful. Another method is to show famous people using the product. If they say that it is good, then many people will believe them and buy the product.

Even if we don't believe everything that an advertisement tells us, we are more likely to choose a product we have seen advertised than a similar one we have never heard of.

Millions of people watch television, so large firms spend huge amounts of money making TV advertisements. These usually last less than a minute, but the songs and slogans can stick in our minds and remind us of the product for years.

"YOUR COUNTRY NEEDS **YOU**"

'Your country needs you'. This powerful poster persuaded many men to fight for Britain in the First World War (1914-18).

USING MACHINES

The telephone

The number of times people use the telephone shows how important it is to communications. In Britain, for example, people make several thousand million calls each year. Most of these calls are to other parts of the country, but we can also dial directly to most parts of the world. Within seconds, we can be speaking to someone thousands of kilometres away. If we keep the message very short, the call can cost less than sending a letter.

When you speak into a telephone, a microphone changes the sound of your speech into electrical signals. Inside the part of the telephone that you hold to your ear is a receiver. Electrical signals from the person who is speaking to you reach the receiver in your telephone. The receiver turns these electrical signals back into the sounds of speech that you hear.

In order to call someone, we have to dial their telephone number, or punch it on a set of buttons. Doing this sends off bursts of electricity, called pulses, along the telephone wires. These pulses work automatic equipment, which connects us to the number we want. If the system does not work as it should, we can ask the operator to try and connect our call.

aerial sending radio waves to satellite

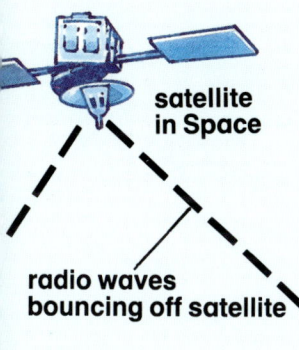

**satellite
in Space**

**radio waves
bouncing off satellite**

For local calls, the telephone signals are carried by cables. Calls over longer distances may also be carried by cable, but often they are beamed from one town to another by radio aerials which are set on high buildings. Some calls to other countries also go by radio.
For calls to distant countries the radio beams may be bounced off a satellite in Space.

aerial

Children in England and Australia wish each other a happy Christmas by telephone. The telephone signals are sent by radio. They are bounced from a satellite high over the equator.

19

Sound and vision

Radio and television are powerful means of communication, because they provide the quickest way of reaching millions of people. Radio and television companies broadcast a wide range of information and entertainment. International news keeps us up-to-date with world events, and we can see pictures of what is happening in other countries. We can even watch astronauts working thousands of kilometres away in Space.

Many programmes that inform us about a subject try to entertain us at the same time. There are also serious programmes for people with special interests, such as science or politics, and they are full of information.

These pictures show how signals picked up by the cameras and microphone are transmitted to your television set, where they are turned back into pictures and sounds.

microphone turns sounds into electrical signals

cameras turn pictures into electrical signals

studio

control room

electrical signals

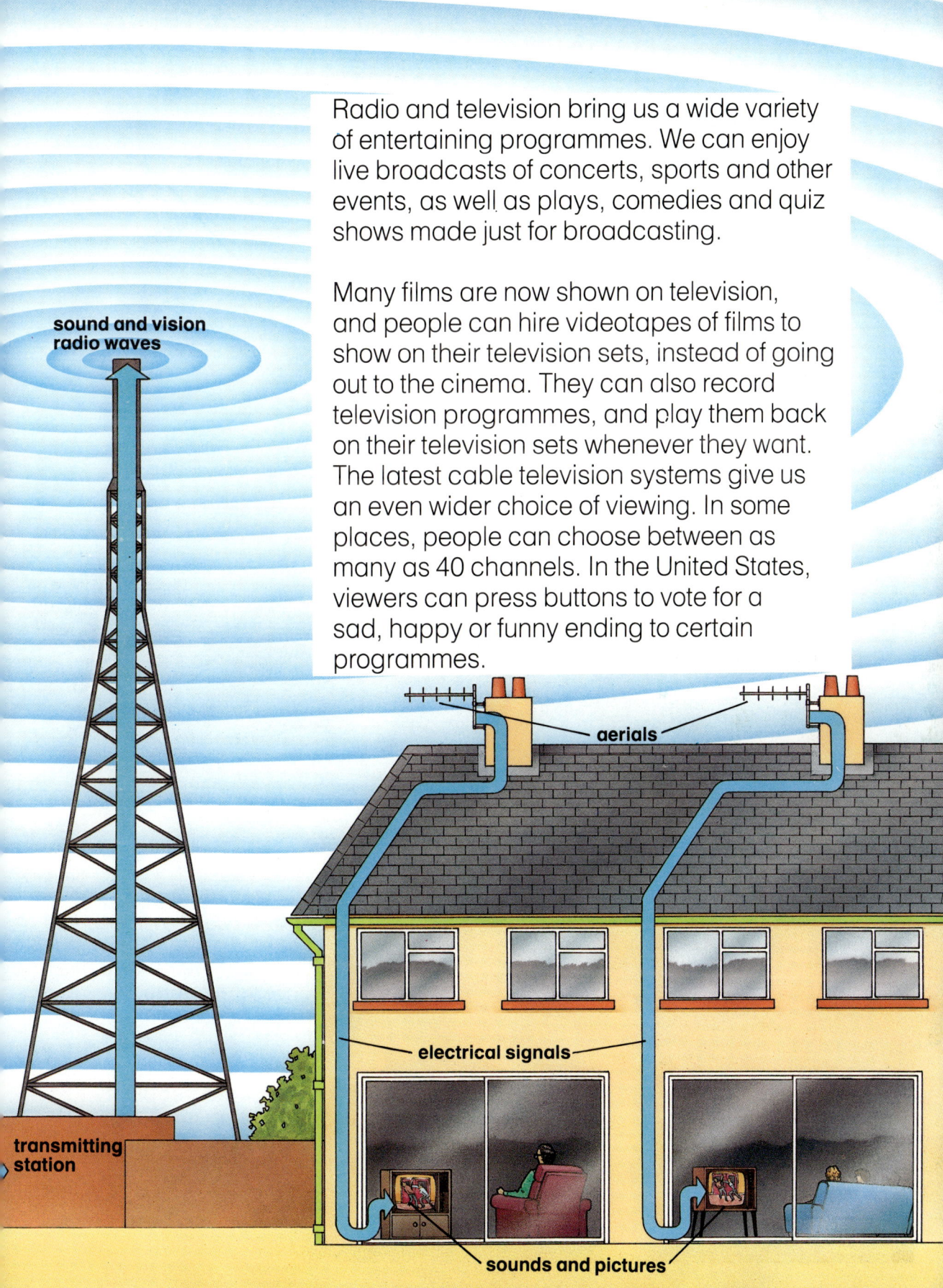

Radio and television bring us a wide variety of entertaining programmes. We can enjoy live broadcasts of concerts, sports and other events, as well as plays, comedies and quiz shows made just for broadcasting.

Many films are now shown on television, and people can hire videotapes of films to show on their television sets, instead of going out to the cinema. They can also record television programmes, and play them back on their television sets whenever they want. The latest cable television systems give us an even wider choice of viewing. In some places, people can choose between as many as 40 channels. In the United States, viewers can press buttons to vote for a sad, happy or funny ending to certain programmes.

sound and vision radio waves

aerials

transmitting station

electrical signals

sounds and pictures

Computers

An electronic computer gives many different kinds of information. It can work out sums, show words on a screen, draw diagrams, control a robot or play games. You have to give the computer special instructions before it can do anything, and these instructions must be given in a way that the computer understands.

Most of the computers that people have at home understand BASIC, a computer language. This is a mixture of ordinary words and special words, numbers and various symbols. It is easier to learn than you might think. The instructions that you give a computer form a program. Programs are also called software. The computer equipment itself is called hardware.

cassette recorder

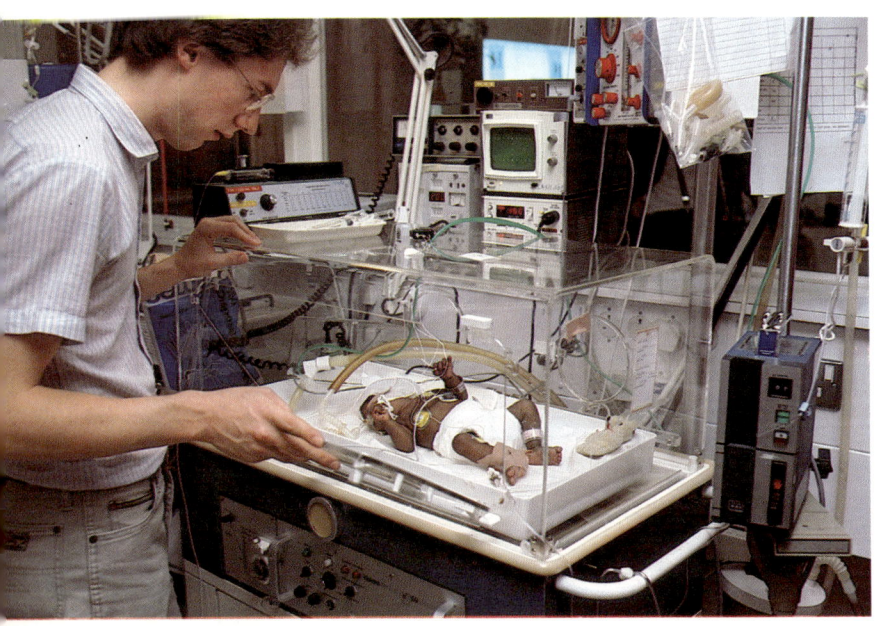

This baby needs special care. A computer makes sure that the right amounts of air and heat get to the baby. Computers also check the baby's heartbeat and other things which can warn people if anything goes wrong.

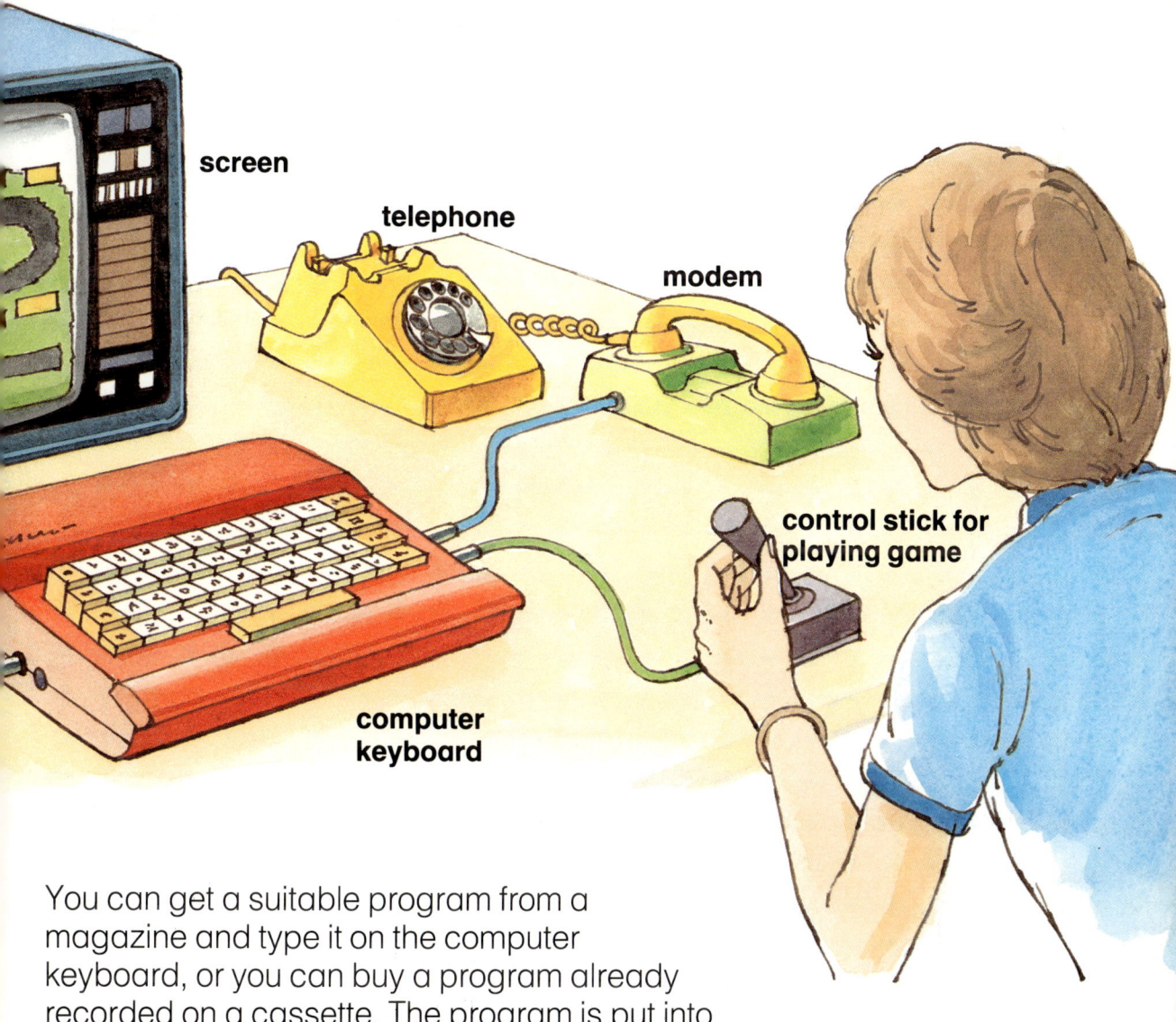

screen

telephone

modem

control stick for playing game

computer keyboard

You can get a suitable program from a magazine and type it on the computer keyboard, or you can buy a program already recorded on a cassette. The program is put into the computer through a recorder connected to it. You can also use a recorder to record programs that you have typed in on the keyboard. Once the computer has been programmed, it is ready to do what you want.

You could learn to write programs for your school or home computer. It could then help with your homework and do other tasks for you, exactly as you tell it to do them.

The program for this child's computer game comes from a computer linked to hers by telephone. A modem changes computer information into signals that can travel by telephone, and changes telephone signals back into computer information.

In the post

Many workers, vehicles and machines are used to get our mail to the right address. Post boxes are emptied several times a day, and the mail is put into sacks and taken by van to a nearby sorting office. There, the mail goes into a large, revolving tube for separation. Slots in the tube allow letters and cards to fall through. Larger items pass along the tube and are dealt with separately.

A machine called a facer arranges the letters and cards so that the sides with stamps on all face the same way. It then prints a postmark over the stamps. Next, the mail passes to coding desks. There, workers type sorting codes on the mail. You may have noticed sorting codes on the letters sent to you. The code appears as a faint line of spots. Sorting machines read the code and separate the mail into piles for each town or district. The piles are then taken to the sorting offices in these areas.

Some trains have a special carriage called a Travelling Post Office. Inside it, mail is sorted into sacks for towns farther along the line. The sacks of mail are unloaded at collecting posts along the way.

The switches and buttons on this electronic sorting machine help it sort 16,000 items per hour into piles for different areas.

Mail for places in the same country is taken mainly by road and rail. Some trains have special carriages for sorting mail, and during the journey mail for an area is sorted into piles for each town on the route. Once the mail arrives at sorting offices in the towns, it is then sorted into bundles for each street, ready for delivery to each home.

Mail for other countries is taken over land, or by sea or air.

A birthday card sent by post can make someone very happy.

Space communication

Many astronomers hardly ever look at stars through a telescope. Instead, they study radio waves coming from Space. These invisible waves are given off by substances in and around the stars. Many stars are so far away that you cannot see them, even through the most powerful telescope, but astronomers can find out lots of information about them by studying radio waves. This method of learning about stars by studying the radio waves they give out is called radio astronomy.

A dish is used to collect the radio waves. This dish, and the equipment connected to it, is called a radio telescope.

A computer has changed the colours on this photograph of Mars. The computer turns slight colour differences into very different colours. This makes it easier for scientists to tell what they are looking at.

Astronomers can send radio waves from a dish on Earth to planets, comets and other bodies in Space. The waves bounce off them and are collected and studied back on Earth. Scientists can then find out how far away a body is, and where it is going. This is called radar astronomy.

Other big dishes beam radio waves to communications satellites in Space. The waves are sent back to dishes on other parts of the Earth. Telephone calls and radio and television programmes can be carried on the waves. In this way, messages and programmes can be sent between any parts of the world, and between Space and the Earth.

Astronaut Robert L. Stewart floats in Space above the American Space Shuttle. All the time he can communicate by radio with astronauts inside the shuttle and with space scientists on Earth. You can see his camera and radio equipment in the photograph.

Future communication

Today, we can connect our computer to the telephone line, and use the line to get information and services from other computers. In the future, many more people will use computers in this way. We may not go out so much, as we will be able to do more things from home. For example, people will be able to connect their home computer to the computers of shops. They can find out what products a certain shop sells, and what they cost. If they wish to buy, they can use their computer to place an order. We will still go to the shops to see and feel some products, but we will use a computer to buy things like food.

Many people will work from home, using a computer linked to others at work. This will save them going into the office. Children may work from a home computer, instead of going to school. Would you like this? Or would you prefer to be at school with your friends?

teaching
computer

central
computer

automatic
lawnmower

satellite receiver dish

'3-D' viewing screen

telephone without wires

...rmation screen ...controls

voice-controlled cooker

A possible home of the future. One central computer may control the heating and lighting, order food, pay bills automatically, and do other household tasks.

As electronic communications improve, people will not need to leave their homes so often. They will not need to talk to other people face to face. So communication between humans may get worse as electronic communications get better. But if people realise how important it is to exchange information, ideas and feelings with others, this need not happen.

GLOSSARY, BOOKS TO READ

A glossary is a word list. This one explains unusual words that are used in this book.

Broadcasting Sending a radio or television programme to the public. The programme itself is called a broadcast.

Cable television A system for sending television programmes into homes through a cable. The cable can carry many programmes.

Facer A machine which arranges cards and letters so that the sides with the stamps all face the same way.

Microphone This changes the sounds of your voice into electrical signals.

Modem This changes computer information into a form which can travel along a telephone line. It also changes received signals back into computer information.

Program A set of instructions that tells a computer what to do. Computer programs are usually known as software.

Pulse A burst of electricity, light, sound or some other signal. Computers and other electronic machines work by means of pulses of electricity.

Radio telescope The dish-shaped aerial and other equipment used to pick up and study radio waves coming from Space.

Radio waves Invisible waves used for radio and television communication. Radio waves are also given off naturally by stars.

Receiver This changes electrical signals into sounds. For example, there is a receiver in a telephone producing the speech that you hear.

Satellite In Space, satellites move around other bodies. The Moon, for example, is a natural satellite of the Earth. Communications satellites are sent into Space from the Earth. They pick up radio signals sent from one part of the Earth and beam them back to another part of the Earth.

BOOKS TO READ
Communication (Visual Books series) by John Bear, Macdonald 1977.
Communication by Kincaid and Coles, Hulton 1976. Lots of interesting projects for you to try.
Computing for Beginners by Keith Wicks, Granada 1983
Information Revolution by Myring and Graham, Usborne 1983. Looks at changes in the ways information is stored and processed.
Telecommunications by Michael J. Barnoo, Wayland 1979. Communications by telephone, radio, television and computer.
Telecommunications (Visual Science series) by John Stevenson, Macdonald, 1984.
Television by Keith Wicks, Granada 1983
Television Studio by Judy Lever, Macdonald 1978.
Television and Video by Helen Mintern, Kingfisher 1983
The Telephone by David Carey, Ladybird 1981.